Poems of a Bering Sea Captain

VOL. II

Poems of a Bering Sea Captain

VOL. II

It's Not What You Think

gatekeeper press

Columbus, Ohio

**POEMS OF A BERING
SEA CAPTAIN**
Vol. II

Published by **Gatekeeper Press**
2167 Stringtown Rd, Suite 109
Columbus, OH 43123-2989
www.GatekeeperPress.com

Library of Congress Control Number: TBD

ISBN (hardcover): 9781662926365
ISBN (paperback): 9781662926372
eISBN: 9781662926389

Contents

Always There

Looking back at what is there
there was never time to care
only time to pay the bills
missing oh so many thrills
times were tough and they looked up
needing you to fill their cup
if you failed all was lost
success came at deadly cost
sacrificed your true intent
trying to pay monthly rent
other bills and constant change
if only you could rearrange
the time it took to get it done
caused you to miss all the fun
they had fun in your absence
then was lost all the chances
to make it up in timely way

have a word can clearly say
all my love was always there
even when seemed not to care
that was only just a ruse
there were very many clues
of the love I have for you
and if you ever wear my shoe
do not lose what means so much
responsibility can be a crutch
do it all in His good measure
will protect your finest treasure
the warm and loving home that is
standing up because of His
never ending thirst for love
our perfect Father from above

Beyond

Beyond your world another lies
it will take you by surprise
what others have experienced
far to painful is it's extent
whatever measure that you gage
is within the enemies rage
in this world that's in your view
nothing is in store for you
the vision that has caught your gaze
will slowly lead into a haze
it happens slow and then gains pace
your soul is the stake you place
careful now this is no game
you will be the one to blame
if you turn away from love
it only comes from God above

Blown Away

Did it seem that I just blew away
seem I had nothing more to say
feel I had no more to offer
no more for you inside my coffer
that just isn't really true
I was feeling really blue
that's no excuse I do admit
I fell deep down into a pit
I fell in it's no excuse
my absence and all the abuse
can I come back is it too late
or have I gone and sealed my fate
shrug that off it's an attack
there's One who always takes back
there is only one sure way
get on your knees it's time to pray

Clarity

What happens when your vision clears
can you get back all the years
what about the souls you hurt
and how you left so cold and curt
can you then explain away
as you slowly walked that day
anything could somehow change
what seemed to be so prearranged
sometimes taken oaths too soon
brings about your sudden doom
wait until you see the sign
of the one who only blinds
that's the time to turn your back
to get protection from attack
this to give up all your sin
means that he will never win
as he tries in vain to steal
God will show you what is real
to deceive and stop your pace
try and make you fall from grace
no descent beyond repair
trust in Him to show His care
slowly as He makes you able
He will seat you at His table
blessing grace unending love
from your Father up above

Commit

As it is I look around
memories keep coming 'round
once were lost within a haze
now I am seeing clearer days
so many lessons dearly paid
lay against the price I paid
to put others before me
hoping for Eternity
no solace or reward did come
from everything that I had done
I was looking far too low
for a dawn that never showed
while I wandered in the dark
He sent to me a vital spark
this it was my final call
just before the final fall
how else could I ever see
all that he wanted from me
until I was broken down
stripped from every earthly crown
those are just a ruse you see
there is only One true Tree
with the fruit you've waited for
and His promised open door
for those who will simply admit
to Him it is you should commit

Explained

Do you have yourself explained
everything you have obtained
all your life and all there is
adds up to an expletive
this world holds too many choices
there are far too many voices
promising a better way
will cause you to fall astray
take unto what you should not
will take away all that you've got
your soul your life and those held dear
lost all to your misguided fear
this world will throw you for a loop
only one way you can recoup
look to the ONE who has the power
to see you through your darkest hour
no other source will ever suffice
to stand up to HIS sacrifice
it is time to unfold your lies
and look through HIS eternal eyes

Final Place

With perspective dearly learned
every time that I was burned
never did my judgement lie
before worthy worldly eyes
I was left as weak and frail
long before my final tale
of all what my life has meant
bending to deceitful intent
It was me the one to blame
and I am most surely sane
judged and unloved left to rust
within this world you cannot trust
even those most close to you
have not even one single clue
to the path for you were made
there can be no Earthly grade
this great value so far exceeds
and can provide all of your needs
even those you've not yet learned
this salvation cannot be earned
just drop down and purely say
to the One you need to pray
I am Yours and in Your grace
put me in my final place

Feeling

I am feeling all my years
reaching to unworthy ears
they are just not ready for
all that is they have in store
and as I see it is their plight
I have for long seen the fight
long before the vision seen
they are living in a dream
made from what they surely know
that leads to an Eternal blow
not it is this for come laid
you are under a deadly blade
do not think your greatness stands
against the only One who plans
an outcome that is far beyond
your so limited Earthly bond
your sights are set way too low
break far away from the flow
that leads to the final choice

do not forget the lightest voice
that leads you to the proper path
and save you from Eternal wrath
this will only come to you
when it is He wants it to
now you're ready for the love
that only comes from up above
now it's time get on your knees
look up to the One who bleeds
for many sins that you now show
and save you from an Eternal blow
the real message is complete
you have a most certain seat
with the Lamb the Son of Men
will see you through your final end
this is the only view that heals
trust in what is beyond appeals

Love's Power

Hatred found an open door
when I was knocked down on the floor
wanting to retaliate
planted deep the seed of hate
years went by and nothing gained
putting others into pain
no hole can be filled with hate
it removes hope of Heaven's gate
your vision stunted and obscure
you need some help you need a cure
this cure it is so freely given
from the only One who's risen
hatred must be left behind
if it is you wish to find
the truth the hope the only way
told to you this long held day
now for you the path is light
leave behind your your blinded sight
give love freely and you'll find

He made you in His gracious mind
your thoughts have been the death of you
His grace and message is the clue
of the way that you should go
that is when your heart will glow
so full of love now nothing left
no room for what you once beset
give your love you now have power
just before your darkest hour
after darkness fades to grace
is when you know you've won the race
He waits for you with loving arms
and will erase all of the harm
that you did within your time
this will be the final rhyme
no judgement here by any man
will ever stand up to His plan

Loudest Whisper

. . .

I am not so good at life
I chose to be under the knife
of this world I tried to please
I should have been down on my knees
I knew the promise early on
never seeing Eternal dawn
that is there and is for us
all the love and if we trust
the message that gives us the choice
you have to lift up your loudest voice
He will hear a whisper clear
inside His Eternal ear
we all need to hold our place
and be steady in this race
some are tested more than you
there is one thing you can do
pray for those you see in pain
your prayers will not be said in vain

*

Make Them Free

What is it that you can do
if it were left up to you
remove the pain from one you care
to lift them high up in the air
far away from the source
and send them on a different course
a new direction filled with hope
and remove the need to cope
with their brutal unfair state
wishing you could change their fate
and could you somehow undo
a vision far beyond your view
the reason why your loved one pains
you only want to hold the reigns
one way you can make them free
happens when you bend your knee

*

Measure Up

What's it like to be despised
you do not measure up to size
they look at you and only see
many sins to a deep degree
these sins they are a part of you
there is an answer always true
the battle to regain your faith
from the clutches of the wraith
deception is a deadly guise
to blind you from Eternal eyes
the light so pale it will raise
with every single word of praise
there is power far beyond
of your limited respond
do not limit your proclaim
of the one Eternal name
He wants to see you strong and bold
not spit you out because you're cold
there is such peace and gentle love
in our Father from above

My Core

I have found my deepest low
it was a tremendous blow
I had to get down to my core
and break away what was before
everything I thought was right
only was to his delight
the evil one who takes away
everyone who's lead astray
it takes a tight and firm compress
to survive the full distress
of losing sight of the One true way
further from each passing day
the road back is long and tough
you will never have enough
if you do not seek the love
that only comes from up above

My Journey

Through this journey that is mine
I have wasted so much time
looking here and looking there
seeking love from anywhere
any place my love was sent
only were my feelings bent
cheated on by lying eyes
to so many no surprise
why did no one let me know
they were ready for the show
just another Jerry episode
quickly soon it would implode
then you finally break away
you have the voice to finally say
this is wrong you do not love
then there comes a vicious shove
pushed away and told you're bad
all of this is very sad
divorce it is a business plan
made for those who try to stand
and do what's right as you were taught
your precious heart has now been bought
fall into the world of men
leads you to a bitter end
just remember when all seems lost
the answer is up on the Cross

Normal

What is normal can you gauge
or are you expressing rage
of a sin that was not yours
that somehow still closed all your doors
the forgiveness and regret
never was the table set
hidden never brought to light
was to the evil one's delight
this and worse was born for years
never reaching open ears
save me from this burden rough
give to me what is enough
to fight and win my chance to say
I needed you Lord every day
when I was lost and far from sight
was when You showed your endless might
now I am back within your fold
and hope to see Your streets of gold
Your promise stands the test of time
for that there is no worthy rhyme
I am just your piece of clay
made to somehow find my way

On The Run

. . .

What is it that you have done
what has put you on the run
far from where the troubles came
leaving you in so much pain
one wrong turn begot another
so far away from your cover
that shields you from the assault
is this really all your fault
your mistake is where the vision was
never seeing feeling sensing love
we all need a place in peace
the enemy will never cease
attack attack against your soul
he wants you in his darkest hole
hid away and lost to hope
hanging from his tested rope
truth and power can smash the lie
and show a true and gracious sky
held together all by Him
has the power to forgive sin
sin is cause and cause enough
the shame you feel is really tough
shame and lies are his game
but is written your Spiritual name
in a book held in His hands
to lead you to His promised land

Perfect Light

How to apply what you have learned
present it well and not be turned
away from sharing precious got
and fight against his deadly plot
shame will be his favorite dart
he will use it from the start
get you cornered and alone
he will cut you to the bone
I have felt the false intent
into his minion I was bent
never giving up my will
blinded losing ever still
more of what you could have done
but even still he has not won
this is no short simple war
he has done this all before
centuries his practice made
hiding deep in darkest shade
bring him to the perfect light
that is when you win the fight
align yourself with THEE true source
that has never lost its course

*

Perspective

. . .

What is perspective I want to know
can it be wrapped in a bow
That is just a fairytale
told to those filled with betrayal
this does not come without pain
there is so much more to gain
beyond your limited worldly eyes
there will be your best surprise
find the truth long written down
will be the only worthy crown
this direction you can trust
all you see then turns to dust
your future is not limited
in any earthly word was said
the Eternal word is the one true way
all it costs is for you to pray

Possibilities

It is painful to see what once was
torn apart with unworthy cause
so much beauty raw and rough
now there is just not enough
time to look back and clearly see
all that was the possibility
of working side by side in trust
it all now is such a bust
there's still hope there always is
if you care deeply for your biz
look to your friend that once did care
and remember when you used to share

Something New

· · ·

What is love how can you know
is it what the others show
or is it something much more dear
this thing that often disappears
or was it even ever there
this thing that hovers in the air
far above for those who reach
a lesson learned and burned so deep
do not compare to those around
all that is that they abound
a prison made by your own hand
and now your mouth is full of sand
this is not what you saw coming
all the while that you were running
from the mess that you had made
you now must accept the grade
of the effort and the care
only One can we compare
His truth has always been the light
to lead you straight to what is right
now there's nothing left to do
you're made into something new

*

Steady Plan

How do I recite the years
to those with unworthy ears
are their ears so poorly made
or are other factors played
unchosen but still pushed upon
they are simply just a pawn
to those living in a hole
and poison their so precious soul
of those exposed and left to seed
are the ones on who he feeds
there is still hope while you breathe
to save you from the Shire Reeve
just say it now the simple phrase
to One who made all days
I am Yours Your molded clay
all it is you need to say
I trust in You the Only One
when coming back You will make done
this creation You perfectly planned
with Your steady Eternal hand

The Path

I do not wish to inflict pain
yet my efforts are in vain
the ones I care for and want to
I fail to show what I can do
where can I find the One true source
please lead me on the proper course
I will need help every day
without could be no other way
to find the path so hard to find
and do it in the knick of time
before it passes the last chance
and you are pierced with final lance
the wound it will be hard to heal
the only cure there is to kneel
give your love and all your faith
will save you from the coming wraith

*

Vision

Somehow I found a way to see
all that was held back from me
I was not ready not in place
I was using too much grace
I learned so much along the way
now given me these words to say
nothing from me has a voice
worthy of His given choice
He gave up all and gladly took
what was foreseen in His book
without His grace we all are lost
beyond His love there is a cost
try to live as you see fit
leads into the darkest pit
no escape once you're there
now is when you need to care
to change the way you live this life
and drop away far from the knife
the blade for you that laid in wait
ever feeding you with hate
stopping love right in its tracks
planning for his next attack
to take away your soul and more
and lead you far from Heavens door
there is the only One true way
get on your knees it's time to pray